SMART-UP
YOUR START-UP

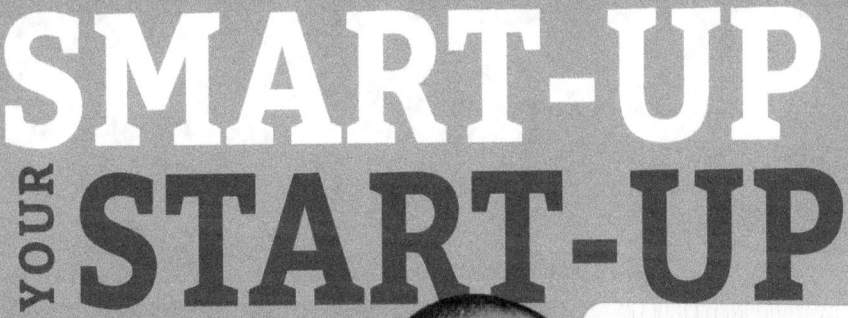

From
Failure
To ## *Success*

By **Salum Awadh**

SMART-UP YOUR START-UP

From Failure To Success

By
Salum Awadh

——————

CONTENTS

1 | The pleasure of starting a business ⑩

2 | The interruptions of business pleasure ㉑

3 | Warning signs of business failure ㉜

4 | The need to smart-up your start-up ㊸

5 | How to smart-up ㉛

    5.1 Finances ㉕

    5.2 Management ㉲

    5.3 Marketing Strategy ㉖

    5.4 Human Resources ㉛

    5.5 Growth Planning ㉝

6 | Sustaining your business pleasure ⑨⓪

How to prioritize your tasks when smarting up

"We emerge from our Cloud of Ambiguity when we are ready or willing to let go of what has held us back."

— Lisa A. Mininni

PREFACE

Every year, hundreds of businesses are established across Africa, and yet majority of them fail just after a few years. Statistics commonly referred to indicates that more than 75% of the businesses fail before reaching their 5th anniversary, this is according to a study conducted by Harvard Business School more than 20 years ago.

 I understand that this most frequently quoted statistics might be outdated or flawed by now, but that's not the question here, the main observation is that many businesses fail after they start or remain small over a very long period of time.

There are many reasons that could explain why such a phenomenon exists, and there are many ways that explain how such a situation can be avoided and allow the business to last with a going concern principle.
This book will look into some of the key factors that cause such a massive failure, how to spot signs of such a failure, and how best we can structure our businesses to be more smarter, efficient, and sustainable.

The chapters of this book will use a metaphor in terms of the titles, but they carry a huge meaning behind them, will see from chapter to chapter. But the thrust of these metaphor is connoted to a scenario of having a pleasure, identifying signs of such pleasure when diminishing, the end of that pleasure, and the possibility of sustaining that pleasure.

The pleasure here refers to a situation when one starts a business, the great feeling of opening the door for customers, the vision, and the feeling of accomplishment, but the question is, how long will that pleasure last?

This book has a total of eight chapters, with chapter one focuses on the processes experienced when one starts a business, and things that need to be put into consideration when starting.

Chapter two looks at the challenges that majority of start-up businesses face, and here the focus is on the immediate challenges that start-up owners experience in their early days of business.

Whereas chapter three focuses on the signs of a business failure, and we should be aware that a business might not necessarily fail overnight, it is a process, and normally there are signs that can be detected.

Chapter four explains the need for you to smart up your start-up, this is the thrust of the book, and the focus here is to help your business avoid business downfall but not fearing failure, failing once is not a problem, but you need to learn from that failure and avoid any further repetitive failures.

Chapter five discusses the "how" of chapter four, because once you understand the need for smarting up your business, the next step is to do it, but how do you do it, this is what this chapter digests for you.

And finally chapter six looks into how you can sustain your business and make it inter-generational, any start-up owner should understand that we start businesses that can outlive us. I hope you will enjoy the book, this book is of interest for those who want to start a business, those who have just started, and those who have been in a business for a longer time but struggling to overcome hurdles of business growth.

"If you can dream it, you can do it"

— **Walt Disney**

1

THE PLEASURE OF STARTING A BUSINESS

It is always a great feeling for someone to start their own business, it brings the feeling of accomplishment, the sense of independence, and the overcome of fear. The combination of these elements create a great pleasure to a new business owner.

But how long that pleasure lasts will much depend on how the business starts, and how visionary is the business owner, if at all the business owner is an entrepreneur, because being a business owner does not necessarily mean being an entrepreneur.

Let me clarify this point of a business owner vs. entrepreneur, there has been a common error in using business owner and entrepreneur interchangeably, to be clear, these are two different people, the former is only someone who has started a business while the latter being someone who possess the characteristics of entrepreneurship such as risk-taking, creativity, and perseverance.

Anyone can be a business owner, but its takes more than owning a business to become an entrepreneur.
And the pleasure of starting a business can be long-term if at all the business owner is an entrepreneur, but business owners who lack entrepreneurship skills are doomed to fail within the very first few years of a business.

Let's see why and how a new entrepreneur becomes excited when starting a business;

The potential to make money

When someone starts a business they believe that there is a huge potential of creating a product or service that can make them financially successful, as the way Robert Kiyosaki put it, "wages pay bills and profits make fortunes". When people look at successful entrepreneurs and how much fortune they have built, they get inspired to start a business, and once they do that, it becomes a great pleasure as the journey unfolds.

The overcome of fear

One of the greatest attributes of an entrepreneur is the ability to overcome fear, that's where it all begins, because the journey to success will never be easier, and overcoming fear as the step to it is the right thing to do. Many people are stuck with their ideas in their minds for fear of going out to start their own businesses. Some fear to lose their steady salary income, some are faced with fear of failure, even though fear is not really, it is just a state of mind. So the day someone overcomes that fear and open the business, what a great pleasure that is.

Sense of independence

Some people believe that the only way to become independent is to start their business and become their own boss. Otherwise, your fate is dependent upon what time you get to work, what time you leave, and how pleased your boss is with you. If fail short of that, your job is on the loop, this kind of uncertainty removes the sense of independence of an individual.

So one of the best ways to become independent is to start a business and be your own boss, and once that is achieved, who can be happier than this entrepreneur?

So with these few issues that can excite the new entrepreneur, the only thing that remains now is how long will this pleasure last, how this entrepreneur will weather the storms of thorny path and mount climbing? One of the best ways is to make this start pleasurable, and most importantly, make it sustainable.

So how can an entrepreneur avoid a false start?

Compliance
The first thing an entrepreneur needs to do for a good start of the business is to be compliant to legal and regulatory requirements of starting a business. I know there are different legislations across the African continent when it comes to regulating the business, but they are common laws when it comes to registering a business and paying taxes.

Make sure that your business is registered with the business registration authority, your registered as a Tax payer and you pay your share of taxes, and your business premise is licensed. The moment you fail to do this, and you start your business behind back doors and skip key compliance issues, you are in a false start, which is as riskier as doing an illegal business.

Market research
Another way to make a good start of your business is to understand the market you want to serve before launching your business, you do not want to enter into a market where there is no niche for you, or the demand is falling, or there is too much regulations that will be expensive for you to enter into that market.

Make sure that you study about the market trends, consumer behavior, and consumption patterns, and if really there is a potential for scaling up your business.

Business plan

It is important for your start-up to be futuristic, you should prepare a business plan. A business plan is a guide that will help you plan for the key components of your business such as marketing, sales strategy, how you will manage your operations, staffing issues, assessing the potential risks of the business you are starting, and most importantly, planning for your finances, in terms of how much capital is needed, how will the business be financed, and forecasting for your future income.

The business plan can be both a simple and technical document, depending on the nature and size of the business you want to start. For example, a business plan to start a boutique worth USD 10,000 can be simple compared to a business plan for a gas exploration project which is worth USD 5 billion.

But the point here is not about the technicality of a business plan but the importance of it. A business plan can even be in bullet points, the point of stress here is on using a business plan as a planning tool, because, as they say, failing to plan is to planning to fail.

A sample business plan outline

Title Page
Name of company, date, contact information, etc.
Table of Contents
Executive Summary
1. Business Concept
2. Company
3. Market Potential
4. Management Team
5. Distinct Competencies
6. Required Funding and its Use
7. Exit Strategy

Main Sections
I. Company Description
- Mission Statement
- Summary of Activity to Date
- Current Stage of Development
- Competencies
- Product or Service
- Description
- Benefits to customer
- Differences from current offerings
- Objectives
- Keys to Success
- Location and Facilities

II. Industry Analysis
- Entry Barriers
- Supply and Distribution
- Technological Factors
- Seasonality
- Economic Influences
- Regulatory Issues

III. Market Analysis
- Definition of Overall Market
- Market Size and Growth
- Market Trends
- Market Segments
- Targeted Segments
- Customer Characteristics
- Customer Needs
- Purchasing Decision Process
- Product Positioning

IV. Competition
- Profiles of Primary Competitors
- Competitors' Products/Services & Market Share
- Competitive Evaluation of Product
- Distinct Competitive Advantage
- Competitive Weaknesses
- Future Competitors

V. Marketing and Sales
- Products Offered
- Pricing
- Distribution
- Promotion
- Advertising and Publicity
- Trade Shows
- Partnerships
- Discounts and Incentives
- Sales Force
- Sales Forecasts

VI. Operations
- Product Development
- Development Team

- Development Costs
- Development Risks
- Manufacturing (if applicable)
- Production Processes
- Production Equipment
- Quality Assurance
- Administration
- Key Suppliers
- Product / Service Delivery
- Customer Service and Support
- Human Resource Plan
- Facilities

VII. Management and Organization
- Management Team
- Open Positions
- Board of Directors
- Key Personnel
- Organizational Chart

VIII. Capitalization and Structure
- Legal Structure of Company
- Present Equity Positions
- Deal Structure
- Exit Strategy

IX. Development and Milestones
Time may be specified on a relative scale rather than specific calendar dates. Milestones may include some or all of the following:
- Financing Commitments
- Product Development Milestones
- Prototype
- Testing
- Launch

- Signing of Significant Contracts
- Achievement of Break-even Performance
- Expansion
- Additional Funding
- Any other significant milestones

X. Risks and Contingencies

Some common risks include:
- Increased competition
- Loss of a key employee
- Suppliers' failure to meet deadlines
- Regulatory changes
- Change in business conditions
- Inflation
- Exchange rate fluctuations

XI. Financial Projections

- Assumptions (Start date, commissions, tax rates, average inventory, sales forecasts, etc.)
- Financial Statements (Balance Sheet, Income Statement, Cash Flow Statement)
- Break Even Analysis
- Key Ratio Projections (quick ratio, current ratio, D/E, D/A, ROE, ROA, working capital)
- Financial Resources
- Financial Strategy

XII. Summary and Conclusions

Appendices May include:
- Management Resumes
- Competitive Analysis
- Sales Projections
- Any other supporting documents

Know your numbers well

There is no way you can have the best start of your business if you cannot explain your business in numbers. Every strategy in a business must also be explained in numbers, and the entrepreneur must be able to demonstrate that. From how much investment is needed for your business to get off the ground, to how much return that investment will generate.

For instance, you should be able to understand the return on investment for using a billboard in advertising over using a TV commercial, you should understand the return on each employee, you should know which product or service makes money, and which one loses money, you should know where your business will be in five years from now, in numbers.

1
- Develop a business idea
- Research your business idea
- Test the viability of your business idea
- Prepare business plan

2
- Register your business
- Procure the basic tools you need for your business such as a computer, a printer etc. Depending on the nature of the business, needs may vary

3
- Launch your business
- Make monthly assessment of your progress Fine-tune your business plan
- Prepare a growth plan

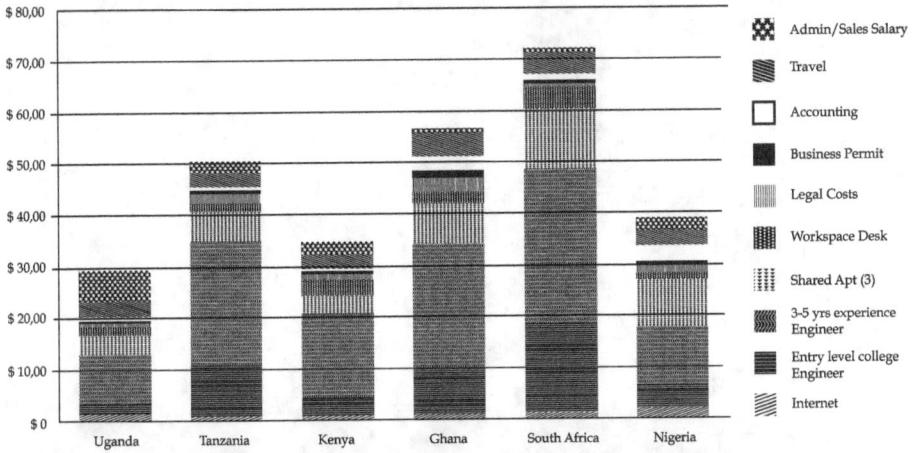

Fisrt Year Startup Costs in 6 African Countries

Legend:
- Admin/Sales Salary
- Travel
- Accounting
- Business Permit
- Legal Costs
- Workspace Desk
- Shared Apt (3)
- 3-5 yrs experience Engineer
- Entry level college Engineer
- Internet

Figure 2: A sample cost structure of starting a tech business in Africa, according to Savannah Fund

---

*"Happiness is not the absence of problems;
it's the ability to deal with them."*

— **Steve Maraboli**

2

CHAPTER TWO
THE INTERRUPTIONS OF BUSINESS PLEASURE

This chapter focuses on the challenges that most start-ups face while trying to build their businesses, just after getting all excited with starting a new business, if the start is not as planned as demonstrated in the previous chapter, one challenge after the other starts to emerge.

Depending on the type and size of the business, challenges that start to emerge vary from case to case, some come as catastrophic as tornadoes, while others spread like lava flow, if these challenges are not addressed the earliest, the interruptions of the pleasure will finally become a total termination of the business existence as fire destroys the forest.

The interruptions of the business appear in different components of your business but mainly in your finances, marketing, management, strategy, and people. These key five (5) selected areas will be the focus of this book, I understand that start-ups face more other challenges, and each challenge worth a separate chapter, but this book will limit itself to these selected areas.

i. Finances

One of the major challenges facing start-ups today is finance. From access to it to the utilization of it. Many start-ups fail either because they can't access enough finance to grow their businesses, or they get the finance and fail to manage it, and for the purpose of the theme of this book, I will not dwell on the access to finance, but rather the management of it.

Most start-ups today fail to separate between their personal from business finances, they keep finances in one account, and as a result, business income caters for non-business expenditure that might have adverse impact on the business cash flow. This can eat up the profit and the core capital of the business, and resultantly, the business starts suffering from cash flow diseases.

One thing most start-ups fail to do is to set aside a salary for themselves, they think as long as they own the business, and when they also think they own success, they forget to learn that success has be earned, with financial discipline at the core. This results into the business owner withdrawing money from the business account with not controls, some even keep their business money into their personal accounts, which they can even draw from the ATM.

Another major financial challenge that starts to interrupt the pleasure is when the business owner fails to keep proper records of the business and personal financial transactions, that ATM transaction will not appear anywhere in financial records of the business.

And even worse, it may reach a point when the business owner cannot even trace the expenditures of the previous month, and this does not bother them because a fraction of start-up owners would bother to hire an independent auditor to look at their books and advise independently. If you cannot trace how much you earned and how much you spent October last year, your pleasure of starting a business is likely to be short-lived.

Table 2: Common mistakes in debt financing

- **COMMON MISTAKES IN DEBT FINANCING**

- **BORROW FOR WRONG REASONS**
- **BORROW WITHOUT PROFESSIONAL ADVICE**
- **FUNDS DIVERGENCE**
- **"COSMETIC" LOANS (FORGING DOCUMENTS WHEN APPLYING FOR A LOAN)**
- **CULTURE OF DEFAULT**
- **NOT ADMIT AND SEEK HELP WITH YOUR FINANCIER WHEN THINGS GO WRONG**

ii. Marketing

One of the common marketing pitfalls of start-ups is to sell a product or service whose market demand is on the decline, and this is a direct result of not doing a market research. The launch of the business can be as delightful especially when initial sales are great and consumers rush for your new product in the market, but that can only be short-lived by the realities of the market dynamics, especially when sells start falling in response to the dipping of the general market demand.

Today if you launch a nice smartphone, some consumers might rush to grab it, but soon as they discover that the phone lacks a front camera for taking selfie, be sure that the demand of your product will be on the decrease sooner than later.

Another marketing challenge most start-ups face is copycat pricing, you bring your product into the market, you see what others charge, and you charge the same. You don't consider your internal factors for proper pricing of your product, you don't ask yourself whether the pricing will cover your costs, or how will it make your product competitive in the mass market or how can it be unique in the premium market, if you do not know about all these, you need to go back to your drawing board.

Some start-ups also go for massive marketing campaign even when their businesses are still as smaller as toddlers, believing that marketing will solve all their sales problems, not even calculating the return on their marketing investment, only to find out that much has been wasted on marketing, and no money coming in, and guess what? Trouble begins.

iii. Management

Management is another key fundamental that if not well done in the beginning, can cause a lot of mishaps to the business.
How is the decision making process done in the business can cause enormous challenges in getting things right as a start-up. Most start-up owners make management decisions without making proper analysis, the so called Cost-Benefit Analysis before a decision is taken, sometimes a financial decision can be better but might cause huge human resources crisis.

Cutting costs, for instance, is better for maximizing profits, but if done on salaries, it can result into lower productivity or even staff turnover, and when the best of your staff start leaving you, you can be sure that the business pleasure is finding its way out too.

The management can also cause a lot of suffocations when the management team which is hired lacks the capacity to manage. Management is both an art and science, poor managers have never been good for any business. Sometimes the start-up owner may hire his/her relatives or close friends regardless of their qualifications and experience on the positions given.

As a result, they start making bad decisions for the business, and since you have emotional connections with them, disciplining them becomes another mountain to climb, while business pleasure is on the downhill.

Management challenges continue to rise as the business owner fails to understand the need and timing of delegation, you find a business growing every month, more staff, more sales, more branches, more customers, the business becomes more bigger but the business owner still wants to hold on, not ready to let go. You fail to delegate when the time is up, you dig your own grave of business failure, as more pending will start piling up, inefficiency increases, and you may start losing customers, leave alone focus.

18 MISTAKES
THAT KILL STARTUPS

1. Single Founder

2. Bad Location

3. Marginal Niche

4. Derivative Idea

5. Obstinacy

6. Hiring Bad Programmers

7. Choosing the Wrong Platform

8. Slowness in Launching

9. Launching Too Early

10. Having No Specific User in Mind

11. Raising Too Little Money

12. Spending Too Much

13. Raising Too Much Money

14. Poor Investor Management

15. Sacrificing Users to (Supposed) Profit

16. Not Wanting to Get Your Hands Dirty

17. Fights Between Founders

18. A Half-Hearted Effort

iv. People issue

If there is one challenge that is not given the deserving weight in many businesses today is human resources. Tanzania, and other many African countries are faced with critical shortage of people with capacity to deliver, colleges and universities produce accountants who cannot even produce a balance sheet, for instance, and you can experience this across all professions. So if you fail to pick the right team from the start, be ready to be the hiring and firing machine.

Most start-ups also have a habit of recruiting cheap manpower who have no quality, have no passion and have no proper mindset, they lack the positive thinking, and the eagerness to learn and grow. They complain a lot, and they want quick results, they think you can just sit beside the river, and the fried fish will jump into their mouth.

Another human resource challenge that most start-ups start facing if they fail to do it right in the beginning is the lack of performance management, the performance of people who are hired in your business must be measured and managed, failing to do so is creating a time bomb, that will explode sooner than later. Start-ups that fail to hire new staff under performance contract, are stuck with non-performing people who become difficult to fire sometimes, or be fired at an additional cost. Once this starts to emerge, you can imagine the stress of the business owner and the pleasure of the business no longer exists.

v. Strategy

Strategy is another critical issue that shapes the future of a start-up, and this is where everything matters, if you are to build an intergenerational business, this is where it all starts. But if you fail to craft a proper strategy for your business, you might be easily swallowed by big guys, you must be able to say why you are in business, and what separates you from the rest.

The business should have a competitive strategy that separates you from mediocre, you don't go into the business to do what others are doing, you are in business because you introduce new solution, you disrupt the market, but if you find yourself on the majority side, ask yourself why are you there, failure of which the change of wind blowing will sweep you away.

The business which is built for intergenerational success must have a succession plan, failure of which, if you die, we burry you with your business in your grave. That will be the end of you and the end of it, and soon more problems will start rising in the company leave behind, and this is all attributed to lack of a succession plan. Who will take over the business after you?, how will the business outlive you?, otherwise, even before you die, especially if it is the family business, conflicts among siblings will start emerging.

A SUMMARY OF THE COMMON CHALLENGES FACING BUSINESSES TODAY "INTERNAL TO THE COMPANY"

- MOST BUSINESS OWNERS LACK ENTREPRENEURIAL SKILLS "YOU THINK OWNING A BUSINESS IS BEING AN ENTREPRENEUR. NO, IS NOT.
- BAD DECISIONS MADE ON DAY ONE OF THE BUSINESS LAUNCH
- POOR OR LACK OF BUSINESS PLANNING
- POOR FINANCIAL MANAGEMENT (FINANCING DECISIONS, PERSONAL FINANCE, LIQUIDITY MANAGEMENT, ETC)
- POOR MARKETING, ACTUALLY LACK OF MARKETING
- LACK OF LEGAL COMPLIANCE & QUALITY CONTROLS
- POOR OR COMPLETE LACK OF RECORD KEEPING SYSTEM
- NO LONG-TERM VISION , LACK OF SUCCESSION PLANNING, AND LACK OF ETHICS

*"Success is not final, failure is not fatal:
it is the courage to continue that counts."*

— **Winston S. Churchill**

3

CHAPTER THREE

WARNING SIGNS OF BUSINESS FAILURE

As these challenges continue to mount on your business, the level of stress increases, and more serious problems start taking shape. And if these challenges are left to transcend to a different level, the survival of the business will only be in a few months, and this is where many businesses die.

But the good news is, once these challenges escalate to a different level, there are normally warning signs, if spotted and addressed, the business will overcome that period, and live on, but if not, the business will be on its way down, and soon that will be the end of it.
So it's very important for an entrepreneur to know these signs and how to spot them, and the forthcoming chapters will discuss about how to address them, smarting up your business, and sustain your business for generations to come.
This chapter focuses only on these warning signs, and once you start experiencing them in your business, know that you need to take quick action, as will be demonstrated in the next two chapters.

These warning signs will again be presented based on our four (4) categories of this book focus, finances, marketing, management, and human resources.

In this way, it will be easier for an entrepreneur to concentrate more on the areas that they believe are of more primary concern to them.

Figure 3: Warning signs and how two different companies respond

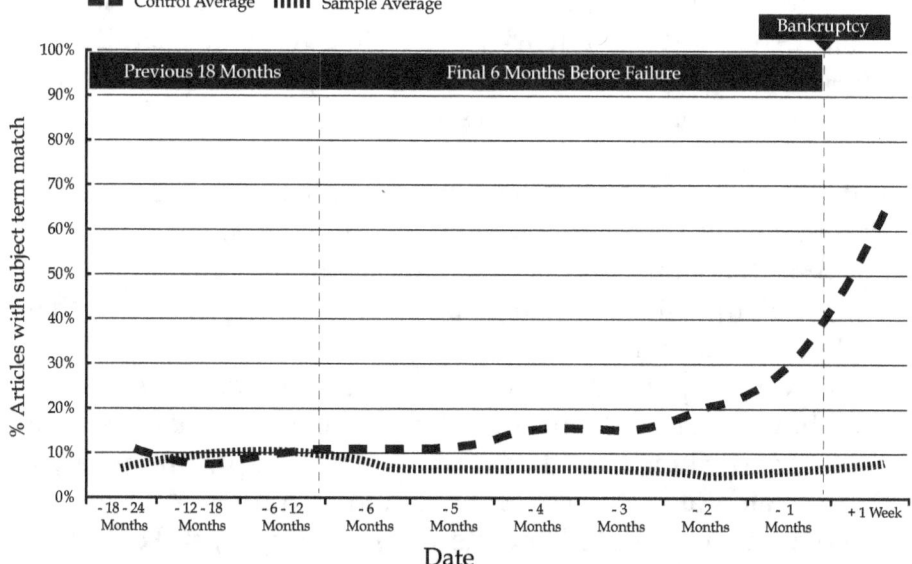

Reference: *A White Paper from LexisNexis and State of Flux Spotting the early warning signs of a company's impending financial collapse*

WARNING SIGNS – FINANCES

Profit declining

One of the major financial signs that a start-up would experience is the falling of profits, this can be very slow or dramatic, depending on what is pulling down the profits. The moment you see this, you need to sit down with your accountant or business advisor and investigate why this is happening, failing to do so, you will only come to realize when you start making losses and it is too bad when you realize this at a late stage.

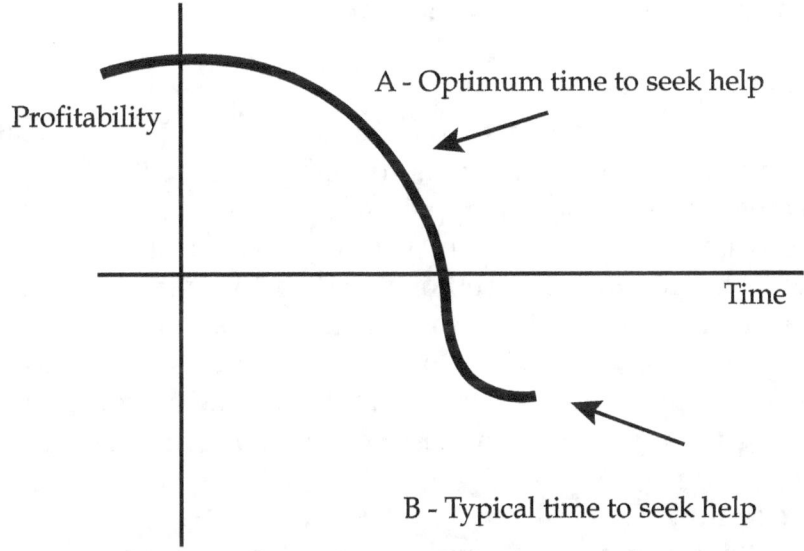

Figure 4: Different points at which start-ups seek help

Liquidity problems

Another sign that your business is on the downfall is when you fail to meet your short-term obligations, now you can't pay your suppliers on time, you can't pay rent on time, and catastrophically you pay salaries by bank overdraft. This is an indication that something is wrong in your business, you need to take action. The biggest sin in business is to run out of cash. CASH IS KING.

Skipping of debt installments

Sometimes you take a loan to start your business or may be along the way you take an overdraft to finance part of your working capital, is all good if well planned. But the moment you start seeing you can't service debt installments on time, and probably your banker starts calling you for a visit, you need to stay upright and investigate what is not happening, because soon worse will be happening.

WARNING SIGNS – MARKETING

Customers leaving

When the business starts you work so hard to grow your customer base, and when things go well, your schedule is full of customers meetings and appointments, and the business is good, right? But the moment you start seeing one customer leaving you for your competitor, you need to pay attention, but unfortunately, most business owners wait until the 6th customer leaves, and this is bad, you need to sit down with your marketing team and find out why. Losing customers is a bad sign for any business, unless you are doing illegal business.

More returns

When the business starts, and customers grow, you see every week more products are shipped out from your shop or warehouse, you see more and more clients lining up for your service. But the problem starts the moment you start experiencing more and more products are being returned, with more complaints from the customers increasing, or your professional reports being returned by your clients multiple times before they are accepted. It's a sign that something is wrong, and if you do nothing, then be ready for anything.

More advertising , less sales

It is expected that when you advertise more and engage more in marketing campaigns that should translate into more sales. But the moment you see no more calls, and sales going down, and even when you add the marketing budget and spend more on advertising, the sales decline is still on the steep slope, you need to take that as a warning sign, that something is wrong and needs a fixing

WARNING SIGNS – HUMAN RESOURCES

Staff turnover

As said earlier, people who work for you have huge impact on your business success, they build great teams, they give more results, and most importantly they get satisfied and they commit themselves to your company. But the moment you start seeing more people leaving your company every year, especially the committed individuals, don't just think is about them, great people rarely leave great companies, so you should take that as a warning that may be something bigger is on the way. Fix it.

Productivity going down

When you start a business and hire your first team, everybody is excited in the company, everybody is happy and hopeful for the company's great future. But as time lapses, you start seeing less results, pending starts piling up on people's desks, deadlines are not met, excuses are becoming a norm, then take that as a sign, something fundamental could be wrong here, either about them, or about the company, or about you.

More fraud cases

When you see more fraud cases in your company, committed by your staff, then you need to know that this is not just about your staff being unethical, but a sign that there are loopholes in your company systems and processes. May be the accounting department is too exposed or the IT system is too weak for fraud.

WARNING SIGNS – MANAGEMENT

Unproductive meetings

As the business owner when building your team, meetings are part and parcel of that process, meetings tend to be a monitoring way to check on the progress of commitments. But when you start experiencing the tendency of meetings generating no desirable results, people just come to meetings as a routine, they don't take notes, and they sleep in the meetings, then stop and ask yourself what is happening, this could be a warning sign of something not revealed to you.

Managers becoming the complainants

When your business starts growing you tend to hire line managers to help you steer the company forward, you expect that these line managers will be on the ground on your behalf, they will supervise and push for more results from the staff. But what happens when these managers become those who complain about work? Give you excuses everyday on failing to meet their targets? Could it be that something is wrong with these managers? Are they not qualified enough for the positions? What is wrong? It is a sign. Take action.

Failing to reach targets

One of the exciting things in starting and running a business is setting up of business growth targets, whether financial, sales, or expansion, targets normally excite every business owner. But this excitement becomes part of business stress when targets are not met, when everything is not coming through as expected. But do you ask yourself why have you been missing your targets for the past 12 months? Could something be wrong with your strategy? It's time to think, it's a sign.

WARNING SIGNS – STRATEGY

No growth at all

You can face all the challenges in your business, from finance to human resources, but if your business is not growing, then know that something is more serious in your business than you can imagine. If your business cannot grow, and it does not bother you, you need to ask yourself why you are in business anyway.

So if after a few years you still at the same position, same revenue, same number of staff, same small office, same product, then is probably time to do a serious thinking and reality check, may be you picked a wrong business or you are not doing it right. I understand business growth is not overnight, but there must signs that there is hope, there are chances for growth, right?

Spreading thin

As the start-up grows, if well-structured with a proper strategy, the growth can be very fast and robust in the very first years, at this stage, the business owner may have more cash at the disposal and can be tempted to open more branches, going global, or starting other businesses, it is better to diversify as you cannot put all the eggs in one basket. But the diversification strategy must be well designed that may not cause any cash problems by spreading too thin, meaning investing in too many small businesses with little investments in each, may cripple al businesses to grow, as they may all remain small, or others dying at the expense of the others.

Failing to adapt

Technology and globalization have made business competiveness very challenging, what appears to be modern today can be outdated overnight by a mere launch of a new technology or a technological update. You can imagine how the mobile technology changed everything, from how we access banking services to how we send money to our loved ones in the village, if you are operating a business in such environments and fail to adapt to these changes, you can as well kiss goodbye your business.

COMMON SIGNS THAT A BUSINESS NEEDS A SMART-UP

Profits going down

Inefficiencies are rampant

High employee & client turnover

Staff are overworked, others are underutilized

Work morale is going down

Business not growing

Old systems no longer work

Debt payments are in arrears

Failure should be our teacher, not our undertaker. Failure is delay, not defeat. It is a temporary detour, not a dead end. Failure is something we can avoid only by saying nothing, doing nothing, and being nothing."

— Denis Waitley

4

CHAPTER FOUR

THE NEED
TO SMART-UP

The gist of this book is to help companies, especially those still in start-up stages to change the way they do business, and establish systems and structures that can help them overcome failure, and get going long-term.

The previous chapters looked in the situation if a start-up is not smart, the types of challenges that can unfold if your business is not smart, the warning signs that can wake you up, and tell you to take.

OPTIONS THAT START-UP OWNERS TAKE
WHEN THE BUSINESS IS NOT SMART

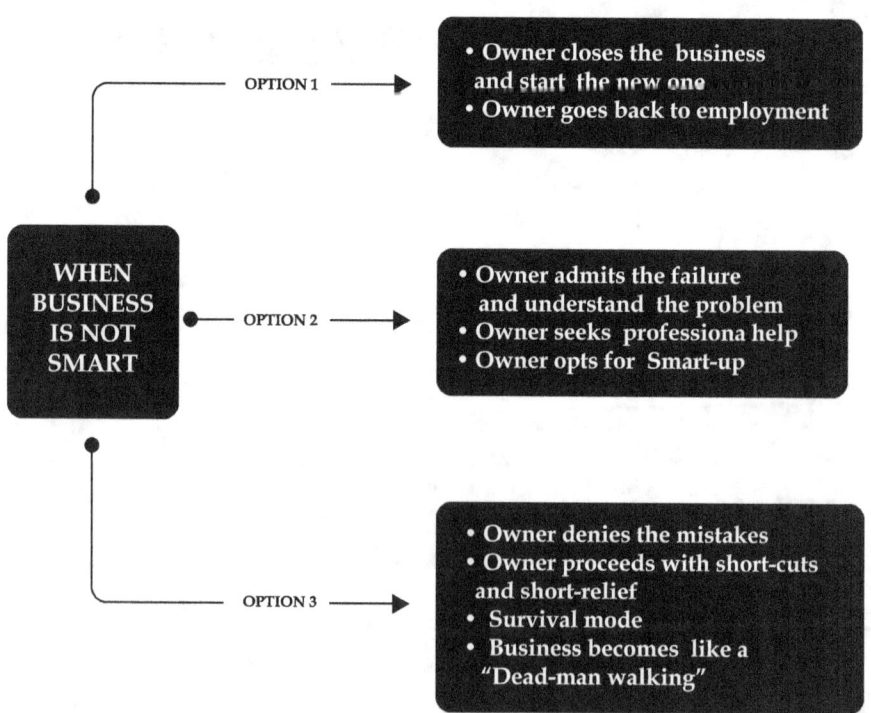

The next chapter will look into how now we can smart-up our businesses, so that they can really become a going concern. But before we get there, this chapter quickly looks into why I think we should smart-up our businesses, as much as we need to address the challenges explained in the previous chapters, but we also need to build long-term businesses proactively.

Embracing and overcoming failure

Statistics indicate that majority of start-ups fail in the first few years after the launch, after investing money, time and energy, you can imagine how devastating failure of your business could be. I know the experts of success say that failure is part of success, but what type of failure? Imagine spending all your life savings to start a business which fails in the next two or three years, but I believe, there are many ways we can prepare our business and withstand such failures, by making our businesses smarter.

If the biggest challenge in your business is the inability to manage cash, which is one of the critical elements of a sustainable business, I believe there are ways that your business can become cash smarter and manage your cash very well and encounter any potential cash flow and liquidity problems that could otherwise put your business in a deep hole.

Withstanding external shocks

When starting and running a business, you should understand that there are internal and external shocks that can send the waves anytime. Internal shocks could be easier to manage as they rise internally, could be due to poor marketing or bad management practices, but external shocks, which can include non-diversifiable risks such as inflation, policy change or exchange rate fluctuations, can be devastating and can put you out of business overnight.

The gist of this book is to help companies, especially those still in start-up stages to change the way they do business, and establish systems and structures that can help them overcome failure, and get going long-term.

The previous chapters looked in the situation if a start-up is not smart, the types of challenges that can unfold if your business is not smart, the warning signs that can wake you up, and tell you to take.

One of the benefits of smarting up your business is to prepare it with a future looking perspective and identify possible risks that a business can face, and how to mitigate them.

Smarting up a business requires you do long-term projections of your business, risk assessment of your business, and most importantly, the succession and contingency plan, doing all these can help you identify potential external shocks and how to handle them when they strike.

Becoming investable and bankable

It is not easy for start-ups, especially in Africa, to access external finance whether in a form of debt or equity. But as the business expands, at some point in time, you will need some external finance to support your growth plans. You may want to launch a new product or project, open a new branch, or increase your production output, and if your internal finances cannot support, you will need to get the right external finance.

But this will not happen with luck, your business must be built in a way that an external financier will find it a viable case and a good investment to put their money into. For this to happen, your business must be operating smartly, must have smart systems and structures that ensure the external financier a good return of their investment over a certain period of time.

Addressing the legal compliance risk

Majority of start-ups start their businesses informally, and only a fraction of them graduate to a formal sector. Operating informally include not filling annual returns, no paying taxes, not filing VAT returns, and the like. This poses them to a non-compliance risk where they face penalties which add costs their business, total closure, or even facing jail term. Smarting up your business looks at all these in the process, smarting up your business means graduating from the informal to formal sector and mitigate the legal and regulatory compliance risk.

Succession plan

When business starts, majority of owners do not foresee how big the business will be, say after 20 0r 30 years, this lack of log-term planning places many businesses at a risk of collapse once the business owner dies, as majority lack a succession plan to ensure that the business outlives them.

Smarting up your business should involve looking at how the business will be handed over to generations after generations, it will require you to design a succession plan while you are there, and start implementing while you are still in control.

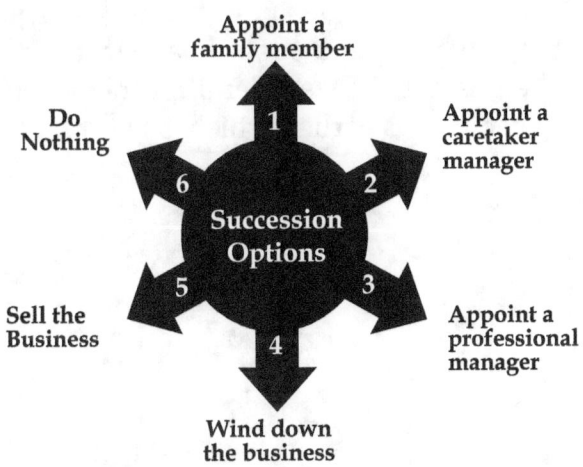

Family Business Succession Options

Family Business Survival Rate

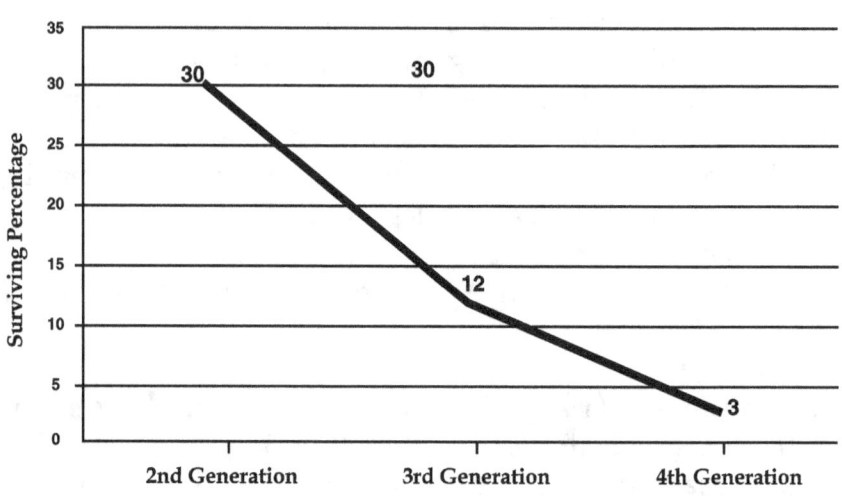

Detecting smoke

Most of the challenges explained in the previous chapters which in most cases result into a business failure occur slowly over time, unless the business owner is able to quickly see the warning signs, short of that, the business will not last. But if you decide to smart up your business, creating a system to detect "smoke" before fire, is, and should be, part of the process, this will help the business owner identifies the challenges and the risk of such challenges earlier, which is better.

Table 4: Guide on how to conduct a health check of your business for an established business

		YES	NO		
1. PRODUCTION/OPERATIONS					
A.	**Purchasing**			MARK	SCORE
i	Does the organization have reliable and reasonably priced suppliers?				
ii	Does the organization have a purchasing program in place?				
B.	**Inventory Control**				
i	Does the organization have effective inventory control policies and procedures?				
ii	Does the organization know our inventory turn?				
iii	Is slow-moving stock managed?				
iv	Have the organization established rational reordering policies?				
C.	**Scheduling**				
i	Do goods and materials move through the business without tieups and problems?				
ii	Does the organization know how long each job should take?				
iii	Have production/operations goals been established, and are work activities aimed at achieving these goals?				
iv	Do production/operations employees use appropriate operations planning and controlling tools and techniques?				

D.	**Quality Control**				
i	Does the organization do well on quality assessments?				
ii	Are inferior incoming materials returned to vendors?				
iii	Are reject rates minimized?				
iv	Does the production/operations process work smoothly and with little disruptions?				
v	Does the organization have a "do it right the first time" policy?				
vi	Has the organization developed any particular competencies in the area of production/operations?				
E.	**Facilities**				
i	Are facilities strategically located close to resources and markets?				
ii	Are facilities, offices, machinery, and equipment in good working condition?				
iii	Does the organization have an appropriate amount of capacity?				
iv	What is the organization safety record?				
F.	**Insurance**				
i	Does the organization have an annual insurance review?				
iii	Are the proper risks covered?				
iii	Does the organization put insurance package out to bid every year?				

2. MARKETING			
A.	**Pricing**		
i	Has the organization priced its products and services appropriately?		
ii	Is the pricing policy based on cost structure?		
iii	Has the organization conducted price sensitivity studies?		
B.	**Market Research**		
i	Is market research used in making marketing decisions?		
ii	Has the organization identified target markets?		
iii	Does the organization segment markets effectively?		
iv	Has the organization identified customer wants/needs?		
v	Does the organization know how the markets perceive products?		
vi	What is the organization's market share, and has it been increasing or decreasing?		
vii	Has the competition been analyzed?		
viii	How is product quality, and how does it compare to competitors?		
ix	Does the organization position itself well against its competitors?		
x	Has the organization taken advantage of market potential?		
C.	**Customer Service**		
i	Is customer service effective compared to competitors?		
ii	Are customer complaints increasing, decreasing, or stable		

iii	Are customer complaint handled effectively and efficiently?		
iv	Is customer service a priority?		
v	Does the organization solicit customer feedback on a regular basis?		
vi	Is there a rational balance between serving customer's needs and good business practice?		
D.	**Advertising and Public Relations**		
i	Is the advertising strategy effective? Website/flyers/brochures, etc		
ii	Are promotion and publicity strategy effective?		
iii	Does the organization select media for measurable results?		
iv	Is advertising consistent?		
v	Does the advertising budget make sense in terms of the level of business and its anticipated, planned growth?		
E.	**Sales Management**		
i	Does the organization have an effective sales force?		
ii	Are salespersons and outside agents properly directed in their duties?		
iii	Does the organization establish individual sales goals?		
iv	Does the organization provide adequate sales support?		
v	Are salespersons well trained?		
F.	**Market Planning**		
i	Does the organization have a marketing budget?		

ii	Does the organization have a marketing plan?		
iii	Do marketing employees use appropriate marketing planning and controlling tools and techniques?		
iv	Has the organization developed any particular competencies in any of the marketing areas?		
v	Has the organization taken advantage of all market opportunities?		
vi	Are present channels of distribution reliable and cost effective?		
3. RESEARCH AND DEVELOPMENT			
i	Does the organization have adequate R&D facilities?		
ii	Are the R&D employees well qualified?		
iii	Does the organization culture encourage creativity and innovation?		
iv	Is communication between R&D and other organizational units effective?		
v	Are the organization's products technologically competitive?		
vi	If patents are appropriate, are patent applications increasing, decreasing, or stable?		
vii	Is development time from concept to actual product appropriate?		
viii	How many new products have been developed during the last year (or whatever time period is most appropriate)?		
ix	Does the organization commit more, the same, or less to R&D than competitors?		
x	Do R&D employees use appropriate R&D tools and techniques?		
xi	Has the organization developed any particular competencies in the R&D area?		

4. FINANCIAL/ACCOUNTING			
A.	**Financial Analysis and Procedures**		
i	Is the organization financially strong or weak according to the financial ratio analyses?		
ii	What are the trends in the organization's financial ratios, and how do these compare to industry trends?		
iii	What is the organization's working capital position? Is it sufficient?		
iv	Are dividend payout policies reasonable?		
v	Does the organization have good relationships with its creditors and shareholders?		
vi	Do financial/accounting employees use appropriate financial/accounting tools and techniques?		
vii	Has the organization developed any particular competencies in the financial/accounting area?		
B.	**Bookkeeping and Accounting**		
i	Are the books adequate?		
ii	Are records easy to access?		
iii	Can the organization get information when the organization needs it?		
iv	Does the organization have monthly P&Ls?		
v	Does the organization have annual financial statements?		
vi	Is your system computerized?		

C.	Budgeting		
i	Has the organization established financial goals? Are they appropriate?		
ii	Does the organization use a cash flow budget?		
iii	Does the organization use deviation analysis monthly?		
iv	Are the organization's capital budgeting procedures effective?		
v	Are capital equipment purchases budgeted?		
vi	Is there a match between the organization's sources and use of funds?		

D.	Cost Control		
i	Are cost items managed?		
ii	Are high cost items treated separately?		
iii	Is the budget used as the primary cost control tool?		

E.	Credit Collection		
i	Does the organization use credit to judiciously increase revenues?		
ii	Does the organization know the credit and collection costs?		
iii	Is the current policy successful?		
iv	Does the organization review credit and collection policies regularly?		
v	Does the organization have a receivables management policy?		

F.	**Raising Money**		
i	Has the organization been successful in raising capital when it was needed?		
ii	Is the organization able to raise short-term capital?		
iii	Is the organization able to raise long-term capital?		
G.	**Dealing with Banks and Other Financial Institutions**		
i	Is the relationship with lead banker open and friendly?		
ii	Does the organization use more than one bank?		
G.	**Cost of Money**		
i	Does the organization compare the cost of money with profit ratios?		
H.	**Use of Specific Tools**		
i	Does the organization know and use break-even analysis?		
ii	Does the organization know and use cash flow projections and analysis?		
iii	Does the organization know and use monthly P&Ls (income statements)?		
iv	Does the organization know and use balance sheets?		
v	Does the organization know and use ratio analysis?		
vi	Does the organization know and use industry operating ratios?		

5. MANAGEMENT			
A.	**Strategic Management**		
i	Do organization employees manage strategically?		
ii	Are organizational goals clear and measurable? Are they communicated to organizational members?		
iii	Is the organization's structure appropriate?		
iv	Is the organization's culture well understood by employees? Does it support organizational goals and mission?		
v	Has the organization developed its vision? What about mission(s)?		
vi	Has the organization developed any competencies in the management area?		
A.	**Record Keeping**		
i	Are records of past transactions and events easy to find?		
ii	Are records retained for at least the minimum legal time period?		
iii	Is access to personnel files limited?		
B.	**Decision Making Process**		
i	Are the organization leaders decisive?		
ii	Is there a decision process (chain of command)?		
iii	Is brainstorming used to generate ideas?		
C.	**Problem Solving Process**		
i	Are there few unresolved problems?		

ii	Is there a problem solving process?		
D.	**Government Regulations**		
i	Is the organization aware of local and national regulations that affect the business?		
ii	Does the organization comply with all regulations?		
iii	Does your organization pay taxes?		
iv	Does your organization remit pension contributions?		
E.	**Leadership and Subordinates**		
i	Does the organization actually take charge of the business and its employees?		
ii	If the organization leaders were to die or be suddenly disabled, is there a ready successor?		
F.	**Business Law**		
i	Does the organization have a working knowledge of applicable business law: contracts, agency, etc.?		
ii	Does the organization know how current contracts and other legal obligations affect the business?		
G.	**Dealing with Professionals**		
i	Does the organization have and use an accountant, attorney, business consultant?		
ii	Does the organization use outside advisors?		

6. HUMAN RESOURCES			
A.	Hiring		
i	Has the right mix of people been hired?		
ii	Does the organization attract appropriate job applicants?		
iii	Are employee selection procedures effective?		
iv	Does the organization maintain a file of qualified applicants?		
v	Has the organization developed any competencies in human resources management activities?		
B.	Training		
i	Does the organization provide employees with appropriate training?		
ii	Are job descriptions and job specifications clear?		
iii	Are jobs effectively designed?		
C.	Motivating People		
i	Do employees appear to enjoy what they are doing?		
ii	What is the level of employee morale?		
iii	What is the level of employee turnover?		
iv	Are organizational compensation and reward programs appropriate?		
D.	Communicating		
i	Are people informed and brought in on decisions?		

ii	Does the organization create opportunities for employees to set their own goals?		
iii	Does the organization effectively use work groups?		
iv	What kind of relationship does the organization have with its employee groups?		

E.	**Enforcing Policies**		
i	Are reviews and evaluations performed on schedule?		
ii	How does the organization treat its employees?		
iii	Are organizational employee discipline and control mechanisms appropriate?		
iv	Are legal guidelines followed in human resources management activities?		

7. INFORMATION SYSTEMS / INFORMATION TECHNOLOGY			
i	How does the organization gather and disseminate information? Is it effective and efficient?		
ii	Is the information system used by employees in making decisions?		
iii	Is information updated regularly?		
iv	Is information distributed effectively and efficiently?		
v	Is information technology used effectively and efficiently in all areas of the organization?		
vi	Do employees have access to contribute input into the information system?		
vii	Has the organization made an investment in information technology that is greater than, equal to, or less than competitors?		

viii	Is the organization's information system secure?		
ix	Is the organization information system user friendly?		
x	Are training workshops or seminars provided for users of the information system?		
xi	Are employees in the information systems/information technology area well qualified?		
xii	Has the organization developed any competencies in the information systems/information technology area?		

8	**RISK MANAGEMENT**		
i	Does your organization have a system to identify measure and mitigate risks?		
ii	How often do you do risk assessment?		
iii	Has your organization suffered any impact of not managing risks?		

*"Take time to deliberate, but when the time for action comes,
stop thinking and go in."*

— **Napoléon Bonaparte**

5

CHAPTER FIVE

HOW TO SMART-UP

After seeing some of the basic mistakes most business owners make right from the time they start, and the types of challenges that emanate from these mistakes, we have seen that if these challenges are not addressed the earliest, the ultimate price is losing the business completely, and what a bad experience would that be for the business owner.

But we have also seen the need to spot warning signs as earlier as possible to avoid any further downgrades, and how these signs can be used as a basis for smarting up your business to be smarter, efficient, and sustainable.

This chapter, which is the centre of the book, explores different ways and strategies that business owners can use to smart-up their businesses, from finances to human resources.

This chapter can be used, in combination with other strategies and experts' opinions, as a way to improve your business or to give you key inputs before starting your business, and avoid any foreseeable failure.

SUB-CHAPTER 5.1 – SMART-UP YOUR FINANCES

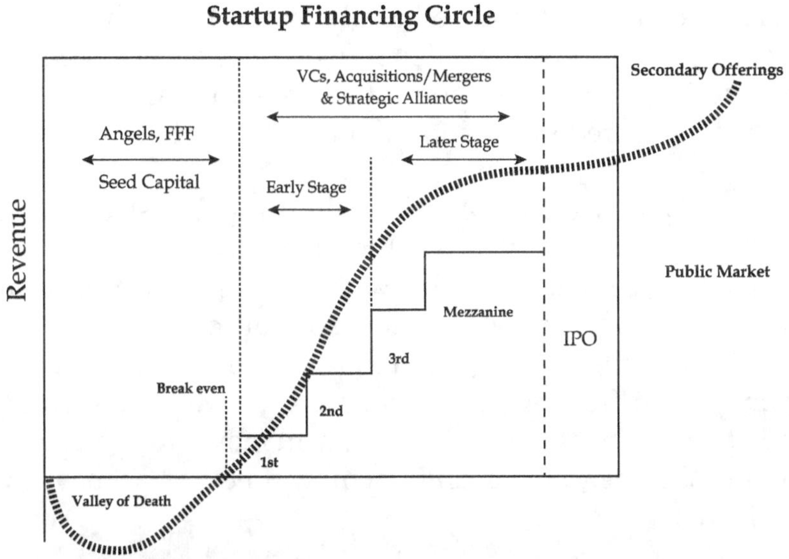

Startup Financing Circle

Figure 5: Starting up cycle with reference to financing

i. Cash control

"Cash is King" is the common statement you can find in hundreds of finance books, it recognizes the key role and position that cash plays in the business, it is clear that without cash, no single business can survive. Without cash you cannot pay salaries, you cannot pay your suppliers, you cannot pay all your bills when are due, simply put, without cash you cannot run a business.

One of the ways you can smart up your cash position is to control it, cash must be controlled in terms of how much comes in and how much goes out, why and when. The business owner must project its cash movements to avoid any type of cash illiquidity position.

There are many ways that you can use to control your cash, but let's see some of these ways a business owner can use to control cash;

• As the business owner, make sure that you get a cash balance position, depending on the level and amount of your transactions, you can have it daily or weekly, or monthly, and the accountant must be able to give you that report whenever required. This will alert you if there are any cash irregularities that you may require action as soon as possible.

• Separate between your personal from business accounts. As the business owner, you need to take a salary, and make sure that there are no uncontrolled withdrawals from your business. As most of business owners do not create a salary for themselves, they end up writing themselves cheque and take money even from ATMs whenever they want, this puts your cash management position at risk, you may fail to keep track of your cash expenditures, and you may quickly start having cash problems.

• You can also reduce cash payments, this reduces the amount of cash at your disposal, you can encourage your customers to do payments directly to your account, or write you a cheque, or do electronic payments, but this can only work if your personal and business accounts are separated.

• Make sure that the duties in handling cash are segregated among individuals in the company, I understand that as a small business it might be difficult to hire more than one person to handle your accounts, either way, whether you can or can't, the point of emphasis here is to make sure that the cash cycle is not handled by one person, who basically receives, records, banks it, prepares bank reconciliation reports, and other reports, this must be segregated.

• Another way to control your cash, which can be abused by fraud, is by knowing the background of the person who handles it. Before you hire an accountant or anyone who will be handling your cash, make sure that you do your background check on this person, you might be hiring a fraudulent person who can cause huge damages on your cash, and it will be too unfortunate when you come to realize about that too late.

ii. Debt management
Debt is one of the ways a business owner can use to finance its business, either in buying fixed assets (equipment, machinery, computers, etc.), or for financing its working capital.
The important issue when it comes to debt is how you manage it, here are some of the ways you can use to manage your debt;

• The first step to manage debt is not taking it at all, before jumping into taking a debt, of any form, make sure that a thorough assessment has been done to establish if there is a really need for debt financing, and whether the company is ready for debt. I have seen some events where a bank approaches the business owner to take a loan after seeing progress of the business, in such circumstances, neither the bank officer nor the business owner conducts any thorough business assessment before the debt is given and that can result into a decision that can be catastrophic

• Understanding of all the costs of the debt, commercial loans in most banks in African charge exorbitant interest rates combined with some charges and penalties that the business owner might not see when taking a loan, I know some other business owners will not take an interest bearing loan because of the faith, but for those who do, they need to understand how devastating these interest rates can be to their businesses, and this is even more serious when it comes to micro finance institutions, imagine today, there are micro finance institutions charging an interest rate of 5% a week, that is equivalent to 20% a month, and a total shocking of 120% per year, that type of debt could be murderous to your business.

• When you have taken a debt, with or without interest, and fails to meet your payment obligations, make sure that you contact your financier as early as possible, explain why you are struggling to meet your payment obligations, and negotiate for a debt restructuring, which may include extended payment period, reduced cost of debt, reduced payment frequencies, etc. Do not start avoiding calls, do not move from your premises without a notice, do not just stay quiet, reach out and negotiate.

• Another way to manage your debt, especially when it starts becoming unbearable is to cut on other overhead costs so you can release some cash for servicing your debt, because the more you skip installments the more debt burden increases. But cutting costs should be done carefully not to affect your efforts to increase your revenue, because you need revenues now more than ever, so be careful the kind of costs you have to cut and their implications on generating your revenues so that it does not become counter-productive for your debt repayments.

iii. Cash flow planning

Cash flow planning is key to success for any start-up, and it all starts from how it is planned, and know that cash flow planning is different from cash control. Cash control is more concerned with managing cash which the company has already earned, while cash flow planning in the context of this book refers to a process of planning for future cash, or simply put, cash flows which are expected by the company.

Cash flow helps the start-up in ensuring that all the payables and receivables are equally matched so the company does not find itself in any liquidity traps, to achieve the proper cash flow planning, the following issues are core to the process;

• When planning for your cash flows make sure that you become as less optimistic as possible, make your cash flow projections in a worst-case scenario, don't expect too much cash inflows too quick, do not plan your expenditures and cash outflows believing that money will just start flowing. Optimism is a bad ingredient for any good cash flow planning.

• The other critical element when planning for your cash flows is to make sure that you do them on a monthly basis, not weekly or annually, the best way to plan and manage your cash flows as a start-up is to do it monthly, most of your expenses will be payable on monthly basis, and income might not be as forthcoming, so you should be able to see how your monthly outflows will be managed if inflows are not timely.

• You need to have one bullet figure for all your expenses that are certain in every month, this bullet figure should always stand out in cash flow planning, alerting you that this figure has to be paid every month, this includes items such as rent, salaries, electricity bills, internet costs, etc. make sure that there is also a stable income stream which should be able to take care of this bullet amount, if the business is not ready to generate inflows, then make sure that you have enough reserves to take you through for at least six to twelve months.

• Consider the market uncertainties whenever planning for your cash flow, there are uncertainties in the market that you cannot control and you cannot precisely predict, so you only need to find a way to accommodate them by adjusting your cash flow planning accordingly. These include things such as inflation, exchange rate, and competitors' price adjustments. You must make sure that your future expected cash flows are adjusted against the expected inflationary and exchange rate changes accordingly.

• Plans for future growth of your business must be factored in your cash flow planning, sometimes you find a start-up planning to open one more branch every quarter, but that is not reflected in the planned cash flows, you should indicate the cash flow implications in that plan, how much investment will need to be paid out, will there be a need to hire more staff, will there be any additional marketing costs, all such items must be reflected in your future cash flows to accommodate for your future growth plans.

iv. Profitability

A business can only sustain loss making or breaking even for only a limited time, then must start making profit, it is the reason why you are in business anyway. In the first years it can be very tough for a business to make profit, but it can even be worse if your business is not as smart when it comes to planning for profitability.

Business profitability must be planned, and here are few issues you can consider when smarting up your business for profitability;

• One key area that drives company's profit increase is reducing your costs, and cutting costs on various wastages that can be discovered in the company, but should not cut cost at the expense of profit drivers or business fundamentals. Some of the areas that you can consider for cost cutting include but not limited to suppliers, unnecessary rental spaces, expensive debt financing, and so on.

• You need to understand what the key drivers of your profitability are, each business has its drivers of profitability. Once you know them, you are in a better position to see how you can boost them, increase their budget, and not temper with them, it could be a certain type of customers, or markets, or product line.

• Another area that you need to look into is the need to increase productivity. One of the critical areas that you can look into is your human resources. People play a key role in increasing profitability of your business by increasing their productivity. You can establish measurements such revenue per employee, output by employee, cost by employee, targets per employee, etc.

• Another important area that you need to work on is the increase of sales, everything starts with sales. You can cut all the wastages, improve your internal processes, provide incentives to your employees, but if you can't take strategic measures to boost your sales, your profitability will always remain low. You can increase you sales by expanding into new markets efficiently, expand your product portfolio, reviewing your pricing, doing up-selling or cross-selling to your existing customers, and so on.

• Depending on the nature of your business, if you are involved with inventory, one key area that you need to smart-up is how you buy from suppliers. You can develop different mechanisms to get best deals from your suppliers. You can make the procurement process as competitive as possible so your supplier can come up with best offers, this can help in reducing your direct costs, and if that can increase your revenue, you can be in a better position to maximize your profitability.

SUB-CHAPTER 5.2 – MANAGEMENT

The role of management starts to be felt the moment the business starts experiencing growth, or when it fails to grow. These are two scenarios where management needs to play a very critical role in growing up the business.

This is another area which the business owner needs to smart-up, some of the key areas that must be considered when smarting up your management are explained here below;

i. Feedback

The management needs to make sure that there is an effective way to get feedback from employees and also give feedback to them. Some of the best practices in improving feedback within the company are explained here below;

• When you start your business and start hiring people, having an open door policy for your employees is as critical as getting feedback from your customers. Make sure that you make it as easier as possible for your staff to approach you and either give their suggestions or express what they feel that can improve the company output

• Hold informal meetings that will provide relaxed atmosphere for staff to start talking, these types of meetings can be held outside the office, you can have staff lunch or night out, and let them mix up with the management team and talk freely, and don't hold people accountable for what they say in these meetings.

• As the business owner you need to understand that feedback is a two-way traffic, you get feedback from employees, and you also give feedback to them. So you can do this by giving feedback to your employees where necessary, and make sure that your feedback is as positive as possible but honest, be specific to the issue or issues, and be hard but not mean.

ii. Team work

Make sure that you create an enabling environment for team work, as the business owner you are also a leader, and you cannot lead if you cannot create a team. These are some of the ways that you can look into when building team work for your staff;

• The first thing you need to do is to understand your team members, know the strengths and weaknesses of each member, know the skills and limitations of each member. This will help you build a team by placing people in their areas of strength with a right mix to build capacity on their weaknesses. This will also help you identify team leaders, and this will also help you know the foot-draggers.

• You should also understand that your employees' lives are not just personal. You can celebrate their important days and accomplishments together, and if you can help their personal problems, be there for them. This creates loyalty and strengthens your team work.

• Another important element of creating effective team work is to clearly define the role and responsibilities of each team member. Let them know the boundary of each member, and what is expected from each one of them.

• Another critical element that you need to consider is to acknowledge the contribution by the team and the team members individually, and create a reward system that will encourage each member to play their roles and responsibilities to the fullest.

iii. Time management

Another critical area that the management needs to smart-up is the management of time, this area is often overlooked, and treated much as a human resource duty, this is rather much of a management issue, that the business owner, as the leader, must build and instil into the people the culture of time management.

Here are some of the ways you can use to create and improve on time management;

• Time management is an art, and every employee include you as a business owner must be able to master effectively. So the very first thing to do will be to organize for a training on time management, you can bring in an expert and train your team on the tools and tips for effective time management.

• Another way to improve time management in your start-up company is to smart up on your automation. You can invest in basic and affordable software that can help save time to a great deal. In accounting for instance, you can invest in an accounting software that can free up a lot of time on data entry or filing in the accounting department if you still have one person taking care of your accounts.

• Another way to improve your time management in smarting up your start-up is to block distractions at work. You can do this by setting the special time for visitors. I understand your marketing or PR person might need to spend some time on social media sites for updating and sharing news with your customers. But various studies have shown that majority of employees spend much time on these sites for non-work activities, you must find ways to limit the use of social media during work hours.

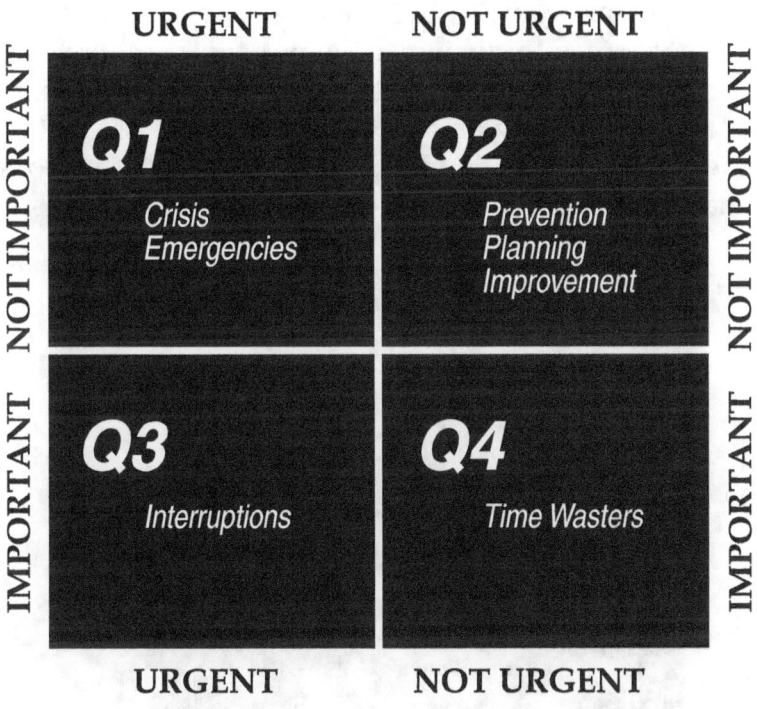

Figure 6: Prioritization Matrix

iv. Change management

While smarting up your start-up you may also need to introduce new changes, there are many cases where employees resist changes or take much time to accept new changes. You may, therefore, need to prepare your team with how to cope and manage the new changes introduced, here are few tips on how to do it;

• Make sure that your team is involved in the process of change management, know that change is not imposed upon people, but must be as much involving as possible. Change which is imposed upon people is normally difficult to attain, faces resistance, and may even cause other people to depart. Use processes such as retreat meetings, employees surveys, and so on.

• Make it clear what is that you want to achieve from the change you are introducing, if your people understand the motives behind the proposed changes, they might buy into the vision and philosophy and be part of the process. Make sure that the change process puts dates, names of who is responsible for what, clear guidelines, milestones, and lines of duties.

KOTTER'S CHANGE MANAGEMENT MODEL

SUB-CHAPTER 5.3 – MARKETING STRATEGY

Another area which is very critical in smarting up your business is on your marketing strategy. If you get it wrong with your marketing strategy, sales may fail to grow, business might be stunted, and cash might fail to come in, and what happens next is to close your business down.

KEY STEPS IN NEW PRODUCT DEVELOPMENT

Idea Generation

Product Screening

Concept Testing

Business Financial Analysis

Product Development

Test Marketing

Commercialization

Smarting up you marketing processes is very key to your business, all great companies have been built on great marketing strategies, from Apple to Coca Cola.

Here are few tips on how to smart up your marketing strategy;

• The first thing you need to do is to define your target market, you cannot just launch a product or service without defining who exactly you are targeting, as that will determine how to develop the key features and benefits of your product or service relevant to your market needs. You can eye for a nice market, segmented market, diversified market, or a mass market, the type of the market you select depends on the product or service you are offering.

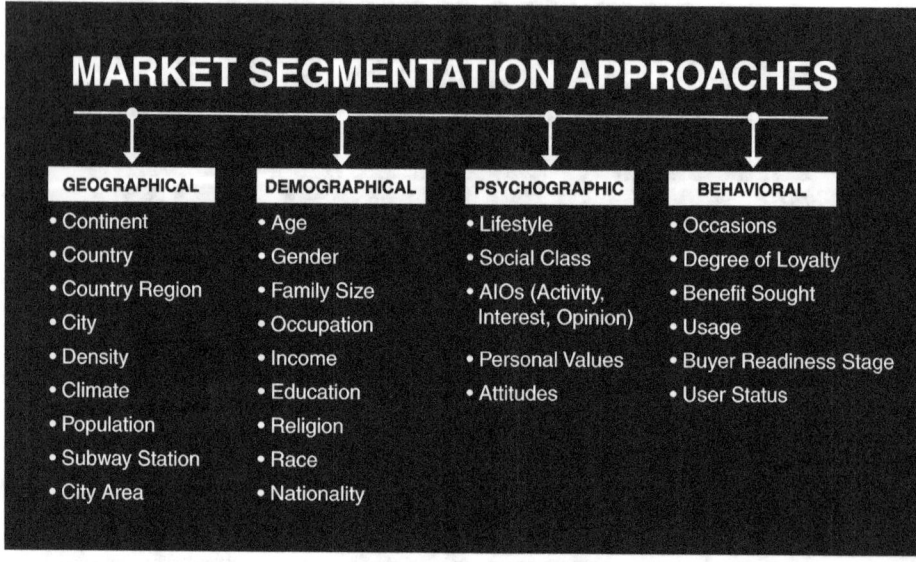

MARKET SEGMENTATION APPROACHES

GEOGRAPHICAL	DEMOGRAPHICAL	PSYCHOGRAPHIC	BEHAVIORAL
• Continent	• Age	• Lifestyle	• Occasions
• Country	• Gender	• Social Class	• Degree of Loyalty
• Country Region	• Family Size	• AIOs (Activity, Interest, Opinion)	• Benefit Sought
• City	• Occupation		• Usage
• Density	• Income	• Personal Values	• Buyer Readiness Stage
• Climate	• Education	• Attitudes	• User Status
• Population	• Religion		
• Subway Station	• Race		
• City Area	• Nationality		

• You need to ask yourself what is your value proposition, which value do you offer to your customers, and how can you differentiate it from other providers, or competitors.

VALUE PROPOSITION

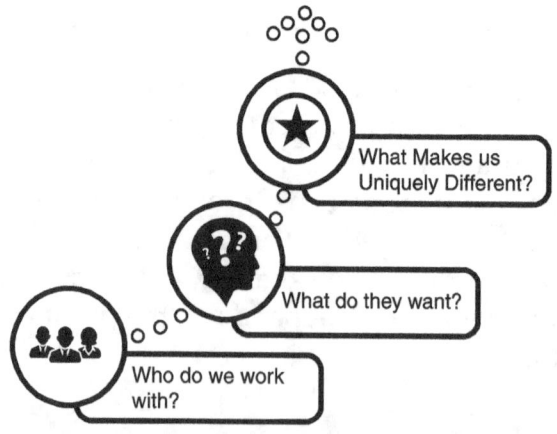

What Makes us Uniquely Different?

What do they want?

Who do we work with?

• Another way to improve your marketing strategy is to find ways to improve your customer relationships. Customers are key to your business success, and for that to happen, they need to feel cared for, and have convenient ways to reach you for feedback. You can adopt things like after-sale service where a customer is cared for even after purchasing a service or product from you, you can also offer dedicated service to your important customers as one of the strategies to retain them. You should always know that a long-term business is built by repeat customers.

• As your start-up grows, you may be exposed to competition, as the competition stiffens you need to find a way to stand out and grow your business. You, therefore, need to develop a long-term competitive edge that will always put you above the rest. You should be in a position where customers can never confuse or substitute your products with your competitors'.

• You can also use the social media effectively and more cost-effectively.

4 STEPS TO SOCIAL MEDIA STRATEGY

---

1 DEFINE YOUR GOALS

2 DEFINE YOUR AUDIENCE

3 DEFINE SUCCESS METRICS

4 EXECUTE. REVIEW. REVISE. EXECUTE

SUB-CHAPTER 5.4 – HUMAN RESOURCES

Human resources is one of the very critical ingredients of a successful and sustainable business, I understand when you start your business you may not be in a position to develop a team, and it as this time when you play a role of a CEO, Accountant, Secretary, Marketing manager, Operations Manager and so on.

You need to know that if you want to grow your business, you cannot do it on your own, you need to develop a great team, and that's where you start seeing people issue as critical, especially when you cannot find the right people to hire.

Or if your start-up has already reached at this stage and you have hired a team, now you are facing a critical issue of getting the right team, hiring and firing has become a norm of the day, this is bad, here are few tips on how best you can improve your human resources;

• The first thing you need to get right is on hiring, many start-up owners complain about having wrong people in their companies, but their hiring process is at fault. They don't hire professionally, not doing objective hiring process, they hire cheap labour, and their hiring process is characterized with nepotism, and so on. Under such circumstances, is not easy to hire a great team if the process of hiring itself is not objective and professional.

• Another human resource challenge that many start-ups face is low productivity of their employees. The effective working hours that majority of employees put into work is quite disturbing, people can effectively work for 3 or 4 hours a day, and the rest of the hours in the day are wasted. One of the ways to smart-up in this area is to introduce performance contract which is connected to one's payment and additional benefits.

• You can also improve the work and productivity of your people by offering meaningful incentives that are also pegged into one's performance, and that goes in tandem with penalties as well, as shall be specified in the performance contract. Employees need to be awarded when doing well, and that drives their productivity.

• You can also provide flexible work options, gone are the days when employees have to physically be on the desk for 8 or 10 hours every day. If you plan well your duties for your team, with clear KPIs, stipulated in the performance contract, you may allow some of your staff like sales and marketing guys to work from remote, give them remote access to office resources. This can help to increase their output.

• Another way to manage people crisis in your start-up company is by outsourcing it to specialized HR companies. If you can get a good HR company which has the internal expertise and experience, you may let them handle all the human resources issues and let you focus on other business strategic issues.

SUB-CHAPTER 5.5 – GROWTH PLANNING

We saw in the previous chapters on why many small businesses fail to grow, and those which try to grow, take a wrong route which become a step-up for their downfall.

This sub-chapter looks at how a small business can plan its growth well, and pursue it in a way that is sustainable, risky but calculated, and incremental. No business is established with no vision to grow, either in terms of product offering, market growth, or manpower.

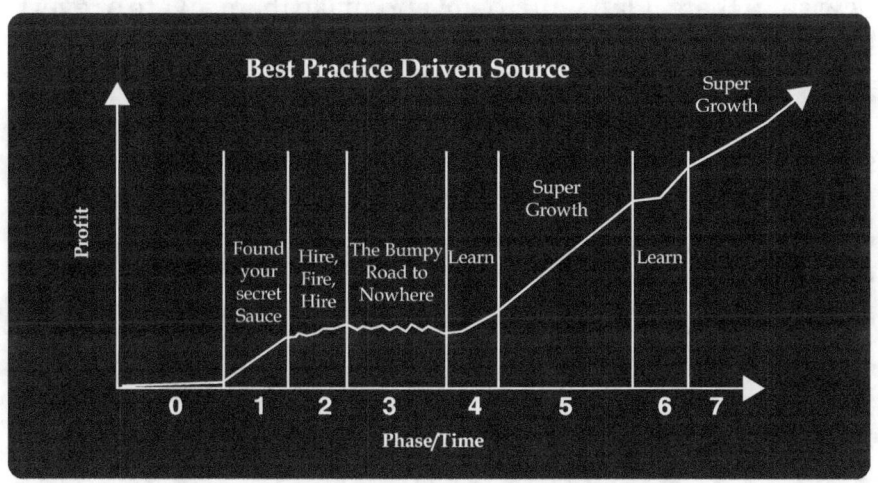

Figure 7: How to plan for your growth over time

When planning for growth, a business owner needs to look at many variables which are key and instrumental in achieving a well-planned growth, here we look at some of them.

Preparing the right team

When planning to grow your start-up from one level to another, you need to make sure that you have the right team in place that will support that growth. If you plan to expand beyond one market, you will definitely need to have enough and right people to serve that new market and customers challenges.

Here are few tips on preparing the right team for your business growth;

• **Awareness:** Do not plan for growth in your bedroom without involving your team, do not let growth comes a surprise to your team. They need to be briefed on growth plans and they need to be aware of what they need to be doing in supporting the planned growth. You do not need your customer service manager to start receiving order calls from another location when she or he has no idea if the business has already set up a new shop there. Plan with them, and make them aware of every step.

• **Additional skills:** You need to understand that when you started your business, the needs and expectations of the company were different, and it is very possible that your team could easily cope with their given skills, but now that you are planning to take your start-up to another level, you may need to assess their skills and do a capacity building where necessary. When the business had a turnover of TZS 50m, the level, type, and complexity of transactions where different from now that you plan to have a turnover of TZS 1 billion, you may need to install an accounting package, an accountant may need to be trained on using it.

• **Build trust:** Planning for growth and building a right team to do that, it is very important that you create an environment of trust among your people. People want to have a feeling of trust that they are trusted and they are able to deliver of what is expected of them. You will also need to start delegating as the company grows, holding into things to yourself just because you don't trust your people will make things even more tougher, learn to trust so you can delegate, and to achieve that you can set up systems and processes that will check and reduce the risk of mistrust and misconducts.

• **Regular meetings:** when planning for growth of your business, there will be new demands and challenges every day, these will need to be addressed as early as possible before they escalate, one of the ways of doing that is to make sure that you meet with your team regularly, and you also create smaller functional teams that can meet for their specific issues without calling the entire staff in meetings which might be of less concern to other members.

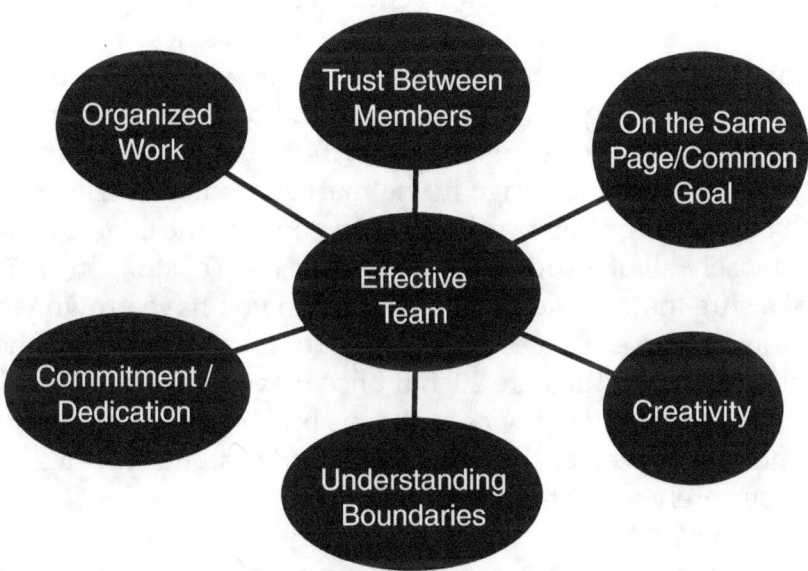

Figure 8: Characteristics of an effective team

Alignment

When your start-up starts growing, you may get emotional and obsessed with growth, and start jumping into new spheres of business which were not originally part of the plan. This can deviate the business from its core and may cause a big mismatch, so there is a need to align new plans with the core guidelines of the business, some of which are explained here.

- **Vision:** the most important checklist of the business is its vision which you developed when you started out. The vision is what guides where the business will be after a certain number of years, so the growth pattern which is developed must be in alignment with the vision of the company. This will help to keep the company in balance with what it aspires to become and what legacy it thrives to create.

- **Competitive edge:** The other important aspect if your start-up business is your competitive edge, what separates you from the rest. The edge that makes your business to be more competitive in the marketplace, without which you may be swallowed by big boys in the market. So when planning for your growth, make sure that everything is in alignment with what gives you a leverage in the market, do not overlook that and become big temporarily because you lack the edge, and fall immensely all of a sudden. If your edge is on customer service, make sure that you keep that even when you have grown your customer abuse. Other start-ups tend to manage well their customers when they are 20, but once they grow into hundreds the whole customer service system is broken down, and profits are not maximized as the expense of good customer service, this will be surely a short-term success.

- **Financing:** in most cases start-ups tend to overlook the financial implications of growth on their finances. You don't just plan to open one shop branch every year without accommodating that cost into your projected cash flows.

Your future cash flows should be reflective of what you plan to do in the future in terms of growth, and that must be aligned into your current planning.
Here are few tips you can consider in ensuring that your growth plans are aligned up with your finances;

a. Seek inputs from your all departments and units in terms of what they will need to support the planned growth, as the start-up owner you may overlook some critical issues that people who are involved in day to day operations may not. Find out what will be the human resources financial needs, the IT financial needs, the marketing financial needs, etc. This will help you understand the more comprehensive picture of financial needs that need to be aligned into your growth plan for the entire company.

b. Explore and understand if there will be any needs to seek external financing, either in a form of debt of equity. Once that is established, start to develop relationships with potential financiers as early as possible. And the type of financing that you will need must be reflected in your financial forecasting and growth plans, if you plan to take up a debt, make sure that your future cash flows have a provision for debt repayments.

c. Start engaging an auditor, sometimes when the business starts growing and more cash is coming in, the owner might not be able to track every transaction, and when the business grows even more, the problem becomes even bigger, is time to engage an external auditor to ensure that all finances are in order and aligned to the planned activities.

Business Model Canvas

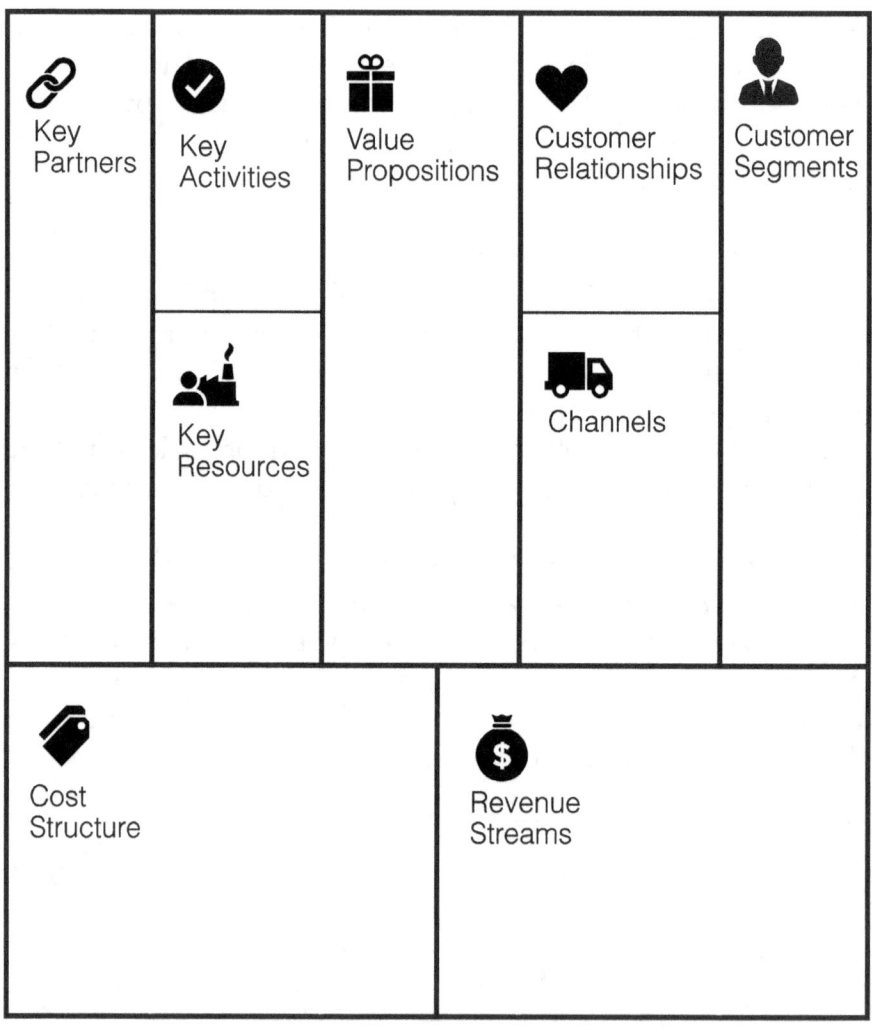

Figure 9: Business Model Canvas to help you plan well

"You will either step forward into growth or you will step back into safety."

— **Abraham Maslow**

6

CHAPTER SIX

SUSTAINING YOUR BUSINESS PLEASURE

Once the start-up is smart enough to operate profitably, the task of sustaining the business, or the pleasure of the star-upt as used in this book, does not end there. The business owner needs to keep on working and ensuring that the work does not stop, growth continues, and the business becomes inter-generational. This chapter looks at some of the ways that a start-up owner can use to sustain the business.

i. Innovativeness

Operating a business today is not as easier as it used be 50 or 60 years ago, with advancement of technology and technological updates happening every day, the business owner needs to keep his eye on the changes in the market, and keep up the pace by innovating continuously.

The business needs to remain as innovative as competitive throughout, the moment the business owner relaxes is when the business can be overwhelmed and overtaken. Look at what happened to Kodak when they could not innovate and change quickly from film to digital photography.

Same thing is happening now with mobile technology and banking services, if banks will fail to keep up and embrace the mobile technology, there will soon become old boys in town.

ii. Succession plan

Another critical element for sustaining a business is by creating a plan that will see the business continue its existence even after you, out-living you, if you cannot do that, then you must be ready to go into the grave with your business. Make sure that the business has systems and processes in place that will make it easier for new people to fill new roles, managers becoming C-executives clearly, nominate the future leader and provide coaching as early possible, and make sure that succession plan is not done as a crisis management tool but strategic initiative.

iii. Cash remains to be the king

As stated in the previous chapters, you always need to know that one of the major reasons why start-ups fail is because they run out of cash. The company that cannot manage to keep itself as liquid as always, and fails to meet its short-term obligations, will soon be out of business, you need to make sure that you plan well you receivables and payables, and cash is well managed. Never run out of cash.

iv. Watch your debt levels

Another related issue that you need to keep your eye on if you want to sustain your business is managing your debt to equity ratio, meaning that you should never let your debts be at levels that are difficult to sustain.

―――――――――――――――――

"Most of us spend too much time on what is urgent and not enough time on what is important."

— **Stephen R. Covey**

COMPLIMENTARY CHAPTER

HOW TO PRIORITIZE YOUR TASKS

As they say, there is no such a thing as being busy but simply lack of prioritization. Planning, as much as it is important for you in achieving your goals, you still need to prioritize and decide what comes first before the other on your to do list of your plan.

Now that you need to dwell on smarting up process, planning for it, and planning it well is as important as the smart business itself. This complimentary chapter is shared to you as guide when planning for your smarting up process.

Many people have plans and ambitions but fail to execute or accomplish them, they have all the resources, they can be as energetic as needed, you can be productive as you may think, but everything comes to the dock when you fail to prioritize.

Prioritization helps you decide what's the most important task to do first and how it impacts on your plans, it helps you allocate your resources effectively, and above all, it helps reduce work stress, as you finish your most important tasks timely and avoid final work rush.

The
Priority Matrix

How Important is the Task ?

LOW IMPORTANCE

Action
Do First

Action
Do Next

LOW IMPORTANCE

Action
Do Later
(If Still Necessary)

Action
Don't Do

HIGH URGENCY

How Urgent is the Task ?

But prioritizing is not as easy as it is said, here are few tips that can help you;

i. Prepare your to do list first

This is the first task you need to do in your prioritization, you don't prioritize what is in your head, you need to write down all the tasks that you want to accomplish in a day, or week, or month, or quarter, or even a year. Then you need to show timelines for such tasks, if resources are needed, and if there is a task that involves another party. This will help you to know what you prioritize can be accomplished with the resources that you have.

ii. Choose what will release your stress

I understand that sometimes some tasks might stress you out and eat all of your energy, it is important that you identify these tasks and put them on your priority list. It is important that you remain focused, energetic, and productive in executing your tasks, but if there is one task that can eat you energy and productivity if not accomplished on time or too quickly, you should know that your whole plan might be in the jeopardy if that task is not accomplished on time.

iii. Be realistic
One of the things that make a lot of people give up on their goals is when they don't see results or impact of what they are doing, and this could be a result of you setting up unachievable goals or taking up a task that you are not able to do or accomplish, so when developing your priority list be as realistic as possible on selecting tasks that are doable, achievable, and can be done within you limited resources. This is very true as well when smarting up your business, can seem stressful in the beginning.

iv. Be flexible
Flexibility is one of the key ingredients of your success, sometimes we plan things in a given circumstance, but circumstances do not stand still, they change, and as they change they might make your work difficult to do. May be there is a payment you were expecting for you to accomplish a certain task, you need to be flexible in a situation when that payment does not come in or when it is delayed.

Finally

You need to understand that starting a business is always an exciting moment, but turning that business into a profitable venture is always a challenge, make sure that you develop right strategies and smart up your business in a way that can be run efficiently and profitably.

You also need to understand that profits that you make can be short-lived, so it is very important for you to explore different ways on how best you can sustain your business.

But this should not make your nervous and risk averse to start a business, do not be afraid to fail when doing, is part of success.

About the Author

Salum Awadh is a renowned business and financial consultant in Tanzania with six (6) years of experience in providing advisory services in the areas of business development, management, finance, investment, transaction advises, venture capital, deal structuring, project management, risk management, socio-economic development, research and training.

He has served a diverse of clients from the government institutions, corporate, international investors, SMEs and not-for-profit institutions in a variety of sectors in Tanzania. Salum also works as a transaction advisor helping Tanzanian companies to raise both equity and debt from regional and global private equity and venture capital firms, advises on divestments, deal structuring, and M&A.

Holding an MBA, he is also certified in the areas of international investment, Islamic Finance, Labor economics, Business development services, Entrepreneurship, Risk management, Corporate Governance, Pension Funds administration, to mention just a few.

He also writes on a personal finance column on the Citizen newspaper in Tanzania with the column titled "Success" every Tuesday, he regularly talks on local TV and radio shows on issues of personal finance entrepreneurship, and economic development

Salum Awadh is also is the author of the book "Dare or Die": The Courage to Pursue your Dream",

Layout Design by Kayitana Ngulu

www.ingramcontent.com/pod-product-compliance
Lightning Source LLC
Chambersburg PA
CBHW052332220526
45472CB00001B/384